# Richard Scarry's
# BUSY TOWN
# BUSY PEOPLE

Random House New York

GROCER BUTCHER BAKER

This is Busytown. My, what a nice town! Busytown is full of busy people. They are all workers. They work hard so that there will be enough food and houses and clothing for their families.

Some workers always do their work at the same place. Others travel from place to place to do their jobs. What does your Daddy do? What does your Mommy do?

a businessman

a secretary

an operator

THE
NEWS

THE
REMARKABLE
BOOK SHOP
E. KRAMER, PROP.

a newspaper editor

a saleslady

a janitor

DANCING SCHOOL

street cleaner

water hydrant

manhole cov

sewer

Sewage

Some workers work indoors,
some work outdoors. Some
work above ground and
some work underground.

wire cable

manhole

There are many workers at Busytown Post Office.

Betsy Bear went to post her Grandma
a birthday letter. She bought an air-mail
stamp and stuck it on the envelope.

She put the letter in the letter slot.

The postmen stamp all the letters with the
postmark of the town they are mailed from.
The address shows where the letter is to go.

The postmaster reads the address on each letter.

All the towns have cubbyholes in Busytown Post Office.

The postmaster puts the letters into the correct cubbyholes. Then he sorts them into mailbags. He takes the mailbags to Busytown Airport.

The mailbag with Grandma's letter
went to Grandma's post office.

Grandma was very happy to get Betsy's letter.

A very busy worker in Busytown is Jason, the mason. Huckle watched Jason and his men build a house. First Jason made a foundation

for the house to be built on. His helper
mixed cement to hold the bricks together.

Sawdust, the carpenter, and his helpers started to build the frame of the house. Jake, the plumber, attached the water and sewer pipes to the main pipes.

I wonder if any children will live there?

water pipe

sewer pipe

Then Jason started work on the chimney.

The men put in
sinks and
toilets and
bathtubs.
They nailed
down floors.

Put th
bath
her

Jason built the chimney higher.

They put a roof and sides on the house.
The electricians
put in electric wires.
All kinds of telephones
were put in.

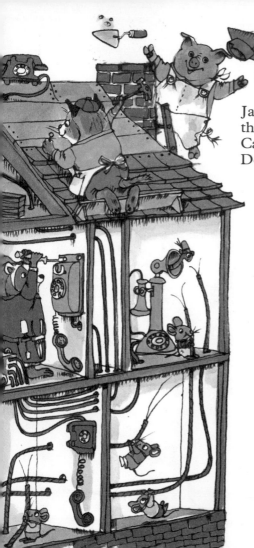

Jason finished
the chimney.
Careful, Jason!
Don't fall!

At Busytown Airport, Huckle was waiting
to fly in an airplane with his Mommy
and Daddy. They were going to visit
Huckle's grandmother.

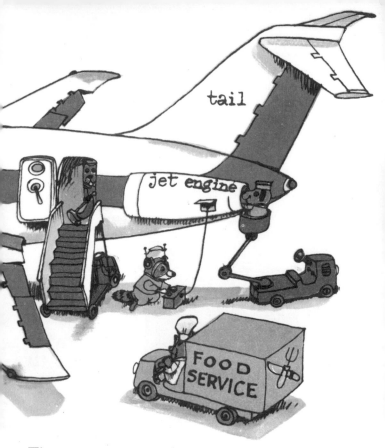

The ground crew was busy getting the
airplane ready to fly.
The family was up on the observation
deck, watching.

When the plane was ready, the flight crew climbed aboard. Then the passengers. After the door was closed, the ground crew took the stairs away.

galley

welcome a

washroom

cabin

The pilot called
the control tower.

cockpit

The man in the control tower said the
runway was clear. Huckle's plane could
take off.

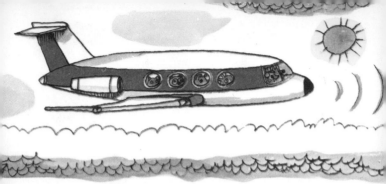

Huckle's plane flew high above the clouds.

The flight attendant served everyone a delicious meal.

Huckle was curious to see
what was in the cockpit.
STOP, HUCKLE!
YOU'RE NOT
SUPPOSED
TO GO IN THERE!
Too late!

COCKPIT
FOR
CREW
MEMBERS
ONLY

FASTEN
SEAT
BELTS

The pilot had started to land. Everyone was too
busy to take Huckle back to his seat.

The pilot slowed down the plane.
He circled lower and lower.
He let down the landing wheels.
The plane came in
for a perfect landing.

Grandma saw Huckle in the pilot's cockpit. "Why, Huckle! When did you learn how to fly an airplane?"

Just outside Busytown is
Farmer Alfalfa's farm.

Farmer Alfalfa likes to grow sweet corn.
Last summer, when it
was time to plant corn,
he planted the seed in
straight rows with his
corn planter.

The hot sun shone down and after a while, tiny green plants popped up.

Rain fell on the plants. Soon ears of corn grew on the cornstalks.

Then—after many days of sun and rain—Alfalfa opened an ear of corn. He wanted to see if it was ready to be picked. It was! The corn was ripe.

Alfalfa picked the corn.
Then he loaded it on to his little old
truck to sell to Grocer Cat.
My! His truck is falling apart!

Well, that's the end of THAT truck!

Grocer Cat gave
Alfalfa money
for the corn.
Alfalfa decided
to buy a new
truck with
the money.

That was his reward
for his hard work.

Busytown needs wood. Out in the forest, many workers are busy cutting down trees.

The tree trunk is sawed into logs.

The logs are put in the river to float downstream.

log

Loggers ride the logs down the river.
They try to keep the logs from getting jammed.
Good work, loggers!
Now the logs can float to the sawmill
and be sawed into boards.

Water falling over
a water wheel makes
the machinery work.

The logs are sawed into rough boards.
The rough wood is sawed into
boards of different sizes.

scrap lumber

FOOLSCAP
PAPER CO.

These boards are called lumber.
Many kinds of workers come to buy this lumber.

Sawdust, the carpenter, uses it to build houses.

BOAT BUILDER

Captain Bill will use it to build a boat.

The road between Busytown and Workville had
been getting bumpy and crooked and very dusty.

The chief road engineer and his many road
builders went to work to fix it.
The surveyor used his instruments to make
sure that the road would be straight.
The surveyor's helpers used stakes and
string to show where the road was to go.
Patrick Pig was busy moving earth with
his tractor shovel.

The stone cutters and the bridge builders
carefully laid stones on the roadbed.

keystone

The road builders used many machines to build the road.

The asphalt was poured into the level finisher, which spread it out flat on the road.

The road was built high in the middle so that rain water would run off into ditches at the sides.

A heavy roller pressed down the
asphalt to make it smooth and hard.

How am I doing,
Chief?

The Busytown policemen work hard
at all times.

In the morning Officer Louie goes home and
Sergeant Murphy reports for duty.

RADIO ROOM

Keep everything
peaceful!

CHIEF

One day Sergeant Murphy was putting tickets
on cars parked where they were not supposed
to be.
Suddenly he got a radio
message from the chief.
A robber had stolen
some bananas!
Look, Murphy!
It's Bananas Gorilla!

CLONK!

OOPS! His motorcycle slipped on a banana peel.
Fortunately he was wearing a crash helmet.

Sergeant Murphy
captured Bananas!

Bananas will stay in jail
until he learns that it
is wrong to steal.

When Policeman Louie comes on duty,
it is time for Murphy to stop working.
He can go home for supper with his family.

Pleasant dreams, Sergeant Murphy! Policeman Louie will keep everything peaceful during the night.